Slaying Job

Fulfilling Law with Grace

Alisa Hope Wagner

Table of Contents

Dedication

Daniel – the man of my dreams

Isaac Jeremiah – my prophet

Levi Daniel – my shepherd

Karis Ruth – my graceful companion

Editing Team – Patricia Coughlin, Faith
Newton, Holly Smith and Daniel Wagner

Albert Morales – my talented illustrator

Holy Spirit – my writing partner

Foreword

Back in 1982 when I was in college, one of my classes was on the book of Job. Actually we spent the entire semester studying this particular book. I wish it would have been possible for this book, *Slaying Job*, to have been included in my class. I am sure had I read the truths Alisa shares within these pages, I would have avoided a lot of unnecessary and self-inflicted pain.

Throughout this book, Alisa expertly breaks down God's work of redemption of humankind within four ages: the age of Noah, of Abraham, of Moses and of Paul. Jesus tells us in John 16:13 that it is the Spirit that will lead us into all truth. Jesus also said it's the truth we experience that we discover our true freedom in Him. (see John 8:32) Well, this book permeates with the revelation of His Spirit and truth. As a result, expect to experience the power of His freedom in your life!

As you prayerfully read these pages, may you discover the rest and redemption found in your "seventh day." May you discover the joy and strength of your "union" with His grace. May you find His peace that comes from realizing the provision He's made for all of your "what-ifs." May you discover His power to live above the passions of the flesh. And, may you experience firsthand the richness of His love for you, as well as His love poured out for others.

Pastor Mike Fehlauer leads New Life Church in Corpus Christi. He has authored four books, the latest being Four Wednesdays in July. He has been a featured contributor to Charisma Magazine, Charisma Leaders, CBN, and has appeared on TBN, Daystar Television and Christian Television Network. Mike has been married to his wife Bonnie for 43 years. They have two children and eight grandchildren and dog named Malachi.

Introduction

> *"**Though He slay me, yet will I trust Him.** Even so, I will defend my own ways before Him"* (Job 13.15 NKJV).

When we get in an argument with God, we are the ones who will lose, and our flesh will be slain. But in our losing, we become more like Christ. He is perfect and holy. We are created in His image, but sin corrupted our perfect form. So as we try to defend ourselves to God, we fail; but in actuality, we triumph because we step into a greater understanding of our need for Him.

Job contended with God. He lost, but in his losing, he won the jackpot of faith. Job found himself in a predicament. He believed he understood God and righteousness. In fact, all the surrounding people saw him as "blameless" (Job 1.1). However, after being stripped of everything, Job finally admitted the truth: "...Surely I spoke about things I did not understand, things too wonderful for me to know" (Job 42.3 NIV). The reality of his imperfections compared to a holy, perfect God caused him to cry out for a Mediator—a valuable glimpse of humans wanting and needing a Messiah—an Intercessor to pull the hands of God into our own, reconciling us to righteousness by faith (Job 9.33).

I too experienced this very long season of contending with God according to my self-perceived, earned righteousness. God had given me promises, and every morning I would go over everything I did wrong and determined to do better. I had to sacrifice more. Work harder. Write more. Stay fit. Be a perfect wife and mother. Otherwise, God would not bless me. I became so fearful of making mistakes that the enemy easily stole my peace and joy. I even dreaded vacations because I knew I would be on the plane headed back home making a list of everything I needed to do to get back into God's good favor (not that I ever left it), so He would not have a reason to withhold His promises.

Slaying Job | Alisa Hope Wagner

Then, I became so sin-focused, trying to earn the promises of God, that I came to a crashing point. I realized after fifteen years of striving to be righteous that I could never live out the holiness and perfection of God. I could not earn a single promise in my own strength, and all my struggling and work through the years were worthless. I lost hope. I wore a heavy cloak of discouragement. I became demoralized to the point that I succumbed to multiple demonic attacks. Demons cannot possess a Christian, but they can feast on the areas not submitted to Christ. And my habit of condemning every little thing I did wrong because I thought they were suppressing God's promises created a large, dark platform for the demon of condemnation, accusation, lies and eventually death to torment me.

Striving to be righteous in my own effort to earn God's promises almost killed me as a mother and a writer. I incorrectly believed that because I was so flawed, God's promises were taking too long to come to fruition. However, all God's promises are "Yes" in Christ, and we should rest in our

"Amen" by faith—no matter how many years pass by as we wait in hope (2 Corinthians 1.20). God's timing for our promises has already been set in eternity and will make their appearance on earth when the time is right. God chooses His timing based on His divine plan alone, and we can't speed it up with our striving.

> *"So humble yourselves under the mighty power of God, and **at the right time** he will lift you up in honor"* (1 Peter 5.6 NLT).

I finally began to allow the Holy Spirit to rewire my brain (thoughts and imaginings), my heart (emotions and feelings) and my will (actions and choices). I wish I could say the Holy Spirit instantly revamped my thoughts and emotions, but it was a long process of deconstructing thought patterns based on ignorance and lies and constructing new thought patterns based on truth and grace. I had to learn how to steward my mind and heart in faith, not fear; and according to grace, not law. I believe if God would have instantly given me

7

the peace and joy I daily pleaded for that I wouldn't have been able to contain them for long. This truth reminds me of the Tent of Meeting that Moses constructed as God's people wandered the wilderness. It wasn't until every detail of this portable Tabernacle and all the furnishings were complete and set in place that God's glory filled it. I needed to go through the process of revamping my inward life for God's glory to fully fill it with His Presence.

> "...So at last Moses finished the work. Then the cloud covered the Tabernacle, and the glory of the Lord filled the Tabernacle" (Exodus 40.33b-34 NLT).

I asked God for a new heart. Not one of stone (law) but one of flesh (grace) (Ezekiel 36.26). And I asked for a renewed mind, one focused on grace, not sin (Romans 12.2). The account of Slaying Job tells a powerful story of the process of deconstructing a life of striving in order to build it back with rest and a double blessing, and we each have our personal Job stories.

Slaying Job | Alisa Hope Wagner

Our stories may have different settings, characters, plots and themes; but they are all about us finally learning to stop striving and enter into the rest of Jesus that He achieved for us on the cross.

> *"There remains, then, a Sabbath-rest for the people of God; **for anyone who enters God's rest also rests from their works,** just as God did from his. Let us, therefore, make every effort to enter that rest, so that no one will perish by following their example of disobedience"* (Hebrews 4.9-11 NIV).

One of the most painful moments of my life can be read in the following poem. I had it all: a wonderful husband, amazing children, beautiful home, time to write – yet I was so depressed, anxious and fearful because of my decades of striving to be perfect. I will never be perfect, but Jesus, in His great love for me, has given me His perfection. He has given it to my husband and to my children. We are holy and righteous in the eyes of all heaven and earth, and no condemnation can fall upon us unless we allow it.

> *"God has united you with Christ Jesus. For our benefit God made him to be wisdom itself. Christ made us right with God; he made us pure and holy, and he freed us from sin"* (1 Corinthians 1.30 NLT).

Here is my award-winning poem about giving up my striving to be perfect and stepping into the righteousness of Christ that is ours by faith.

Slaying Job | Alisa Hope Wagner

Breaking the Religious Spirit
Alisa Hope Wagner

Promises too lofty for me to reach.
Underserving. Lacking. Never enough.

What can I fix?
What can I change?
What can I learn?
What can I erase?

Analyzing,
Repenting,
Striving,
Condemning,
Self-loathing –
Never enough.

Joy vanishes behind false righteousness.
Peace dissolves behind discouragement.

The enemy creeps in.
Makes a home in my pain.

Slaying Job | Alisa Hope Wagner

And a bed in my fear.
Builds a system of torment in my mind.

Promises too lofty for me to reach.
Damnation punctures my heart.
My soul bleeds out.
And death replaces hope.

Demons laugh and lie.
I listen. I examine. Nothing computes.
The racket rages around me.
My inner screams can't compete.

"Quiet yourself," God gently whispers.

No! No! The lies slice!

"Quiet yourself," He repeats.

It hurts! Make them stop!

God, Where is Your Peace?
Where is Your Joy?
Where are Your Promises?

"Trust me. And quiet yourself."

Slaying Job | Alisa Hope Wagner

The lies blare on as I sit silently.
Each like an old record, spinning an evil
noise. Louder and louder until the clashing
becomes a single static whine.

"What do you hear?" He asks.

I sense it now, as God sits with me in the
shadows.

The lies create distractions,
Desperately disguising a singular truth:
Satan's seething, supernatural aversion for
me.

he hates my design by God.
he hates my destiny from God.
he hates my dependency on God.

Discouragement begets condemnation.
Condemnation begets lies.
And lies beget death.

I'm dismantling the system of torment.
Piece by putrid piece.
Lie by vile lie.
Until joy overcomes with His righteousness.

Slaying Job | Alisa Hope Wagner

And peace overshadows discouragement.

Promises are too lofty.
But they are gifts for me.
I can't earn them.
I can only believe.

Finally, my striving dies in the arms of faith.
Jesus is enough.

Slaying Job | Alisa Hope Wagner

Illustration by Albert Morales

Desired Mediator

The Repent of Righteousness

"In the land of Uz there lived a man whose name was Job. This man was blameless and upright; he feared God and shunned evil" (Job 1.1 NIV).

The *Book of Job* is a true story with a lot of mystery. It may be the oldest book of the Bible. It may have been written by Moses. It may have occurred during the time of Abraham. But no one truly knows. Very little is known about Job's ancestry, as well. What we know about him comes from his poetic, heart-wrenching tale of loss and restoration. What we can confirm, however, is that Job was a real man. He was mentioned by name in Ezekiel 14.14 and James 5.11. Also, the Apostle Paul referenced the *Book of Job* twice in Romans 11.35 and 1 Corinthians 3.19. Moreover, the *Book of Job* is referenced in multiple Old Testament books, including Jeremiah, Psalms, Proverbs and Isaiah. Needless to say, the *Book of Job* had and still has a powerful influence over Bible readers. But why?

The *Book of Job* was written in three parts: **Introduction, controversy and conclusion**. Some stories are plot-driven and some stories are character-driven. The *Book of Job* is a character-driven poetic story with a massive character arc of its main character, Job. A character arc happens when a character goes through something difficult and transforms from beginning to end— becoming wiser, stronger, merciful, grateful, loving, etc. This is what happened to Job.

The interesting, and rather beautiful, aspect of his character arc is that he went from "blameless" to "despised," which may seem counterproductive but is actually the most precious conversion that can take place.

Slaying Job | Alisa Hope Wagner

"My ears had heard of you but now my eyes have seen you. Therefore I despise myself and repent in dust and ashes" Job 42.5 -6 NIV).

Because no human righteousness, no matter how many weeds of sin we see and pull daily, will ever match the righteousness of the Messiah given to us freely, pulling out every weed of sin all at once by faith. No matter how "good" we think we are, we are despised without Jesus' righteousness, and Job was about to learn this imperative lesson. His righteousness could not even come close to the righteousness of God. Job had to transform from being a sin-focused man to a grace-focused man.

Introduction: A Righteous Spirit

Job was known as a rich and righteous man from the East with seven sons, three daughters and a great wealth of livestock. He was "blameless and upright; he feared God and shunned evil" (Job 1.1 NIV). After his children would have feasted on their birthdays, Job would make sacrifices for them just in case they sinned (Job 1.5).

At first, Job's sacrifices for his children seem righteous and good, but the motive behind his sacrifices makes a bold statement: Job was sin-focused. He had created a custom in his heart to fear even the "perhaps" of sin. He didn't attend the parties with his family. He had no idea what they were doing, so he sacrificed based on what-ifs. That is one sign of a sin-focused person. They fear sin so much that they shut out relationships and celebrations because people are messy and in need of love, acceptance and, most importantly, a Savior. Being around imperfect people may get our "righteous" feet a little dirty. But as Jesus rightly said: *"Those who have had a bath [salvation] need only to wash their feet; their whole body is clean. And you are clean..."* (John 13.10 NIV).

Yes, walking with Jesus and loving His people will get our feet dirty, but He is always there with His towel around His waist ready to clean our grimy feet as we follow His heart of love. Fear of sin will stop us from loving people, so we can stay clean in our own eyes. But if our eyes are full of Jesus, we will see that we have already been made clean by His Finished Work on the Cross.

> *"Our sins are washed away and we are made clean because Christ gave His own body as a gift to God. He did this once for all time"* (Hebrews 10.10 NLV)

Why did Job make sacrifices to purify the what-if sins of his children? The precedent of sacrificing to atone for sin occurred in the Garden of Eden after Adam and Eve sinned against God.

> *"The LORD **God made garments of skin** for Adam and his wife and clothed them"* (Genesis 3.21 NIV).

God sacrificed an animal, so He could cover the shame of Adam and Eve. They were given only one command at that time (unlike the 613 commands given to Moses many generations later). I can imagine that Adam and Eve weren't perfect. I bet they got angry at each other or complained sometimes. But there were no laws or commands against those things because the Lord walked with them daily. He had a relationship with them, and He could teach and guide them like a good mother and father would with young children. However, He did establish one single commandment:

> *"And the LORD God commanded the man, saying, 'Of every tree of the garden you may freely eat; but of the tree of the knowledge of good and evil you shall not eat, for in the day that you eat of it you shall surely die'"* (Genesis 2.16-17 NKJV).

Just think of that. They could have everything in the garden except that one tree. In essence, that tree became a blessing and a curse. It was a blessing because the Tree of Knowledge of Good and Evil symbolized our free will to choose. God truly created us in His image as sons and daughters with an independent ability and will to decide. But it's a curse because Adam and Eve both ate from the tree and sin entered the world.

Slaying Job | Alisa Hope Wagner

Thankfully, God already had a two-part plan in place to redeem the mistakes we make with our free will and to perfect what we create with our free will. This two-part plan included an added day (the Seventh Day) and an added tree (Tree of Life). After God created all six days, He claimed that they were good: *"Then God saw everything that He had made, and indeed it was very good. So the evening and the morning were the sixth day"* (Genesis 1.31 NKJV). However, He knew He would be giving His children free will, so He created an extra day where He rested, and Jesus (The Tree of Life and Lord of the Sabbath) would make His sacrifice to restore all six days back to God (Matthew 12.8, Revelation 2.7 & 2 Corinthians 5.19).

Once Adam and Eve sinned, they saw their shame. Now they knew the difference between good and evil. They tried to cover up their shame in their human effort with fig leaves, but God covered them with the skins of animals—thereby making the first sacrifice to atone for sin. But this sacrifice would only be a foreshadowing of the sacrifice Jesus would make to atone for all sin (once and for all) on the Seventh Day of

22

Sabbath. And that is the single most profound truth that Job discovered during his ordeal. As he was stripped of all his human righteousness (fig leaves), he realized finally that he needed a Mediator between God and him—not a sacrifice from animals where he constantly had to focus on the what-ifs of sin, but a once-and-for-all sacrifice that would bring him and his family back into relationship with God no matter how often they messed up.

> *"For He is not a man, as I am, That I may answer Him, And that we should go to court together. Nor is there any **mediator** between us, Who may lay his hand on us both. Let Him take His rod away from me, And do not let dread of Him terrify me (Job 9.32-34 NKJV).*

Job finally realized—after chapters and chapters of defending his righteousness—that he could not contend with God, and he finally repented of his incorrect belief system. He had to lose everything to gain a deeper understanding of God and His great grace. But once he clung to this new awareness, God was able to fill his life with even more of His blessings and glory.

Discussion or Journal Question

Our lives can be at times plot-driven (external forces moving our story along) or character-driven (internal forces moving our story along). Can you think of a plot-driven moment in your life and a character-driven moment? What did you learn? What do you believe God was achieving during those times? Write your answer below or discuss with a group.

Parable of Fathers

The Father Who Runs

Old Testament Father:

"His sons used to go [in turn] and feast in the house of each one on his day, and they would send word and invite their three sisters to eat and drink with them. When the days of their feasting were over, Job would send [for them] and consecrate them, rising early in the morning and offering burnt offerings according to the number of them all; for Job said, 'It may be that my sons have sinned and cursed God in their hearts.' Job

did this at all [such] times" (Job 1.4-5 AMP).

We can infer at least six things from these two above verses. First, Job's children were close and enjoyed celebrating and feasting together as a family. Second, it is not mentioned that Job was invited to these parties, so perhaps he did not enjoy or he may have even disapproved of these celebrations. Third, Job feared that his children would sin at these parties and sent for them when they were done. Fourth, Job would sacrifice offerings to atone for the sins his kids might have committed. Fifth, Job thought the worst—that his kids might have cursed God. And sixth, Job believed he had the power to dictate his children's righteousness through his own efforts of sacrifice.

Therefore, and I'm using creative license here, I'm seeing Scripture paint a picture of grown kids enjoying life and not inviting their father to their feasts because he was so fearful that they would say or do something wrong. However, they would indulge him once the celebrations were over by abating his fears and allowing him to "purify" them just in case they weren't perfect. Instead of simply showing mercy toward his kids' pre-conceived imperfections, Job gave sacrifices, which seems to contradict the very words of Jesus.

> *"But go and learn what this means: 'I desire mercy, not sacrifice.' For I have not come to call the righteous, but sinners"* (Matthew 9.13 NIV).

I truly believe that Job did all of this out of a love that reflected his pre-transformation character arc. He strove to be righteous in his own efforts before God, and his striving encompassed his children, as well. However, the what-if sins he focused on finally became a reality, and he was confronted with the very thing he feared the most. God gave Satan permission to take everything from Job—children, wealth and health—except his very life (Job 1.12 & Job 2.6-7). I assume Satan left Job's wife alive because she would become the mouthpiece for his true evil desire: For Job to curse God.

"His wife said to him, 'Are you still maintaining your integrity? **Curse God and die!**' He replied, 'You are talking like a foolish woman. Shall we accept good from God, and not trouble?' In all this, Job did not sin in what he said" (Job 2.9-10 NIV).

Thankfully, Job never did curse God, but he did have a bone to pick with Him. The *Book of Job* from chapters three to thirty-one accounts of Job arguing his innocence with three of his friends: Eliphaz, Bildad and Zophar. But his friends finally quit arguing with Job because *"he was righteous in his own eyes"* (Job 32.1) They believed he had done something wrong to deserve the misery he was in, but Job vehemently said he had done everything right. Both parties were missing the point. We all fall short of the glory of God, and only the sacrifice of Jesus can make us right.

> *"This righteousness is given through faith in Jesus Christ to all who believe. There is no difference between Jew and Gentile, for all have sinned and*

fall short of the glory of God, and all are justified freely by his grace through the redemption that came by Christ Jesus" (Romans 3.22-24 NIV).

New Testament Father:

"The son said to him, 'Father, I have sinned against heaven and against you. I am no longer worthy to be called your son.' But the father said to his servants, 'Quick! Bring the best robe and put it on him. Put a ring on his finger and sandals on his feet. Bring the fattened calf and kill it. Let's have a feast and celebrate. For this son of mine was dead and is alive again; he was lost and is found.' So they began to celebrate" (Luke 15.21-24 NIV).

I only added a few verses of the "Parable of the Prodigal Son" (Luke 15.11-32) in this section, but I will reference verses from the parable as they arise. Again, we can infer at least six things from the parable. First, like Job, the son believed he was worthy, which was illustrated when he demanded his inheritance as a son (Luke 15.12). Second, the father gave the inheritance willingly to his son knowing he would sin. Third, after the son lost everything (Luke 15.14), he experienced a character arc and realized that all the good he had in his life came from his father, not his own efforts. Fourth, unlike Job, the father didn't fetch his son to come to him. Instead, this father ran to his son with compassion, hugging and kissing him (Luke 15.20). Fifth, the father loved to celebrate with his family, ordering his servants to prepare a great feast. And sixth, the father also made a sacrifice for his son; but this sacrifice (a fattened calf for the feast) was not done out of a what-if-my-son-sinned fear, but from a heart of love and joy that his son had returned.

Now, again using creative license, I see two fathers who both look righteous at the outside, but which one is the true picture of our Heavenly Father? It isn't Job because his tactics obviously failed. He lost every single one of his children whom he constantly fretted and sacrificed over.

Slaying Job | Alisa Hope Wagner

(However, his story will not end there as we will later discover. His character arc will not only change him as a man but as a father). No, the righteous father is the father of the prodigal son who is an image of our Heavenly Father. God is merciful, forgiving, slow to anger, joyful, celebratory, and He initiates extremely generous relationships. He gives generously, and He doesn't need to constantly make sacrifices for our sins because He added an extra day and an extra tree for Jesus' Final Sacrifice when He created the world.

God is joyfully resting in the Sabbath of Christ, seeing us, His sons and daughters, as perfected and holy through the sacrifice of Jesus, the Messiah, and Redeemer of the world. We have a Holy Father Who runs to us with open arms, hugs and kisses us, adorns us with His royal attire (Job 15.22), and celebrates with us! He doesn't fear our what-if sins because they have been wiped clean through the Finished Work of Jesus Christ. We can rejoice once we accept Jesus as our Lord and Savior because we can return to our Father's home as beloved righteous heirs.

Slaying Job | Alisa Hope Wagner

"Now if we are children, then we are heirs—heirs of God and co-heirs with Christ, if indeed we share in his sufferings in order that we may also share in his glory" (Romans 8.17 NIV).

If you haven't accepted Jesus, the Messiah as your Lord and Savior. I invite you to pray the prayer below, so you can become a true son or daughter of God. I know it may sound simple, but the Bible says that *"If you declare with your mouth, 'Jesus is Lord,' and believe in your heart that God raised him from the dead, you will be saved"* (Romans 10.9 NIV).

Salvation Prayer:

"Father God, I know I am not righteous. I could never have a relationship with You without a Mediator, the Messiah. Jesus took my sins to the Cross and gave me His righteousness, so I could be reconciled back to You, my Heavenly Father. I accept Jesus' sacrifice for me and invite Him into my heart and life as my Lord and Savior. I want to be completely clean once and for all with the

33

Slaying Job | Alisa Hope Wagner

Blood of Your Sacrifice. I ask now for Your Holy Spirit to fill me, guide me and bless me with Your goodness. Thank You, Father God, for saving me from a life of constant striving to be worthy. My worth is found in Your Son alone. I pray this in Jesus' name. Amen."

Discussion or Journal Question

As parents or influential figures in other people's lives, we may have played both the parental figure of Job and the parental figure of the Father of the Prodigal Son. Or we may have had experiences with our own parents and/or parental figures playing more strongly in one role over the other. Think of a time that one or both parental figure metaphors have affected your life. Write your answer below or discuss with a group.

Character Arc

Obstacles of Change

"We can rejoice, too, when we run into problems and trials, for we know that they help us develop endurance. And endurance develops strength of character, and character strengthens our confident hope of salvation. And this hope will not lead to disappointment. For we know how dearly God loves us, because he has given us the Holy Spirit to fill our hearts with his love" (Romans 5.3-5 NLT).

The Controversy: The Breaking

Why does God allow adversities to come into our lives? First, we must evaluate whether these problems are hitting us because of our own unwise choices or if they are opportunities sent to us by God which will allow our character to grow and change. However, even when we mess up, God can use ALL THINGS (including our mess-ups) for our good because we love Him (Romans 8.28). God sent Jesus to the desert to be tempted by Satan to test His character (Matthew 4.1). Therefore, out of obedience, God may call us into the wilderness of our own lives because He knows that's where the miracle of change occurs.

Paul says to "...*rejoice, too, when you run into problems and trials*" because they help build our character. We must remember this life is much like the womb of a mother. We are developing into the people we will be for eternity once our body dies. We do not develop during easy, comfortable times. We develop during the winds of pressure and the waves of resistance.

Slaying Job | Alisa Hope Wagner

Much like a gym, the world is filled with countless workout machines, aerobic classes and free weights (all metaphors for difficult people, situations and seasons) that if we obey the leading of the Holy Spirit, will build our souls—minds (thoughts and imaginings), hearts (emotions and feelings) and wills (actions and choices). Plus, as we die to self (our understandings, our wills, our desires, etc.), the Holy Spirit will have more room in our lives to fill us with His goodness, power, fruit, blessings and healing.

> "Because of the LORD's great love we are not consumed, for his compassions never fail. They are new every morning; great is your faithfulness. I say to myself, 'The LORD is my portion; therefore I will wait for him.' The LORD is good to those whose hope is in him, to the one who seeks him; it is good to **wait quietly for the salvation of the LORD**" (Lamentations 3.22-26 NIV).

Slaying Job | Alisa Hope Wagner

Job experienced such a wilderness where he had to *"wait quietly for the salvation of the Lord."* In fact, on a scale of 1-10 of difficulty (1 being a slight hiccup and 10 being the Work of Jesus on the Cross), Job's wilderness experience may be considered a 9. Job lost everything including his health, and his wife pretty much told him to drop dead (Job 2.9). It's obvious that they must have not had a tightly knitted relationship for her to show no compassion. Furthermore, his friends were determined to expose what he did wrong to deserve such destruction. However, his wilderness experience wasn't due to his wrong choices; rather, God allowed this wilderness experience to upgrade Job's understanding, which then upgraded his life.

The Conclusion: The Doubling

> *"The LORD blessed the latter part of Job's life more than the former part. He had fourteen thousand sheep, six thousand camels, a thousand yoke of oxen and a thousand donkeys. And he*

also had seven sons and three daughters" (Job 42.12 NIV).

Once Job overcame the obstacle of losing everything, his understanding of God was renewed and transformed. God spent four chapters of the *Book of Job* explaining and dialoguing with Job about how it was impossible to "contend" and "correct" Him (Job 40.2). God is perfect in every way, and when we wrestle with Him, we will lose; but in the end, once we repent, we will ultimately win. Job had no clue that being wise in his own eyes was not looked at favorably by God (Job 37.24). Job's efforts of righteousness without relationship were much like what Jesus said about the righteousness of the religious leaders of His time.

"But I warn you—unless your righteousness is better than the righteousness of the teachers of religious law and the Pharisees, you will never enter the Kingdom of Heaven!" (Matthew 5.20 NLT).

Slaying Job | Alisa Hope Wagner

The teachers of religious law were considered the most righteous people of their time, but their righteousness was based on human effort and performance. Jesus explained that not even they were righteous enough to enter heaven, which is why we need the Mediator, Jesus the Messiah. This is also why our relationship with God far outweighs our religious understanding of God.

It took losing everything for Job to discover that his thinking was backward. Instead of trying to earn God's favor through his constant sin-focused efforts, he should have been seeking friendship with God. This way he could freely live in God's favor by resting with God, not striving for Him. Abraham was called a "Friend of God," which is the highest calling for us all (James 2.23). The problem was that Job couldn't live out what he didn't understand—meaning we cannot live a life we are unable to imagine or experience. Job had to wrestle with God to forge a true relationship with Him, not one based on rumor and hearsay. I know from experience that wrestling is an intimate, passionate sport where someone loses and someone wins, but both parties experience a moment of bonding.

> "I had heard of You [only] by the hearing of the ear, But now my [spiritual] eye **sees** You. 'Therefore I retract [my words and hate myself] And I repent in dust and ashes'" (Job 42.5-6 AMP).

Finally, in the end, Job fathered seven more sons and three more daughters. Plus, God doubled everything he owned. He went from 7,000 sheep to 14,000 sheep; 3,000 camels to 6,000 camels; 500 yoke of oxen to 1,000 yoke of oxen; and 500 female donkeys to 1,000 female donkeys. And it is interesting to note that none of his servants was mentioned in the second half of his life; though, I'm sure he had many. He had a very large number of servants for the first half of his life and would need even more with his growing estate. Instead of mentioning his servants, however, what was mentioned was his family.

Once the ordeal of his adversity was over, his sisters, brothers and friends from all over feasted with him and comforted him. Can you imagine it? Job was actually participating in the celebration! Job the perfect, upright man who always interceded on the behalf of others was now being given sympathy. Not only that, his family and friends gave him gifts of gold in order to kick-start his renewed prosperity (Job 42.11). He didn't earn these gifts. They were given to him freely and now his success was not based on his own efforts but on the grace of others. Truly, the righteous man Job had been humbled, and God greatly blessed him (1 Peter 5.6). And his love for his family is so apparent that he even gave his daughters (which was an extremely unusual practice for his time) an inheritance of his estate. Finally, he died seeing and enjoying his family to the fourth generation.

> *"Job lived 140 years after that, living to **see** four generations of his children and grandchildren"* (Job 42.16 NLT).

That word "see" in the above verse is the same root word for the word Job uses when he finally *sees* God in Job 42.5. This word comes from the Hebrew word, *rā'â*, which means among other things, to behold, to respect, to consider, to regard, to enjoy, to distinguish and to give attention to. Needless to say, relationships had become a large part of Job's life. Instead of being sin-focused and keeping others at a distance, he had now become grace-focused and invited others (with their mistakes, struggles, hang-ups and messiness) into his life.

Just like Job, God will allow us to go through the fires of persecution to bring us to a higher understanding of His love and grace. God has a character arc in mind for each of us. He wants us to mature to the "full and complete standard of Christ." And it is only through trials that we shall grow, mature and rise above.

> *"This will continue until we all come to such unity in our faith and knowledge of God's Son that we will be mature in the Lord, measuring up to the **full and complete standard of Christ"** (Ephesians 4.13 NLT).

Slaying Job | Alisa Hope Wagner

I look back at my Job experience and thank God for it. Though at the time I couldn't understand why God was allowing me to go through the fires of persecution, I can now see today just how much I have gained. My understanding and need for God have more than doubled. Scriptures I once only had "heard" about I now "see," according to the Hebrew word, rā'â. I have greater mercy and compassion for people who are experiencing difficulty. I have taken authority over my mind and heart. I know better how to steward my thoughts and feelings. Instead of waking up each morning criticizing myself, I wake up thanking Jesus for His righteousness which is mine by faith. I tell God all the wonderful blessings for which I am grateful. And God made me this promise: "Not even the aroma of smoke will be left."

In the story of Shadrach, Meshack and Abed-Nego, they were bound up and thrown into the furnace for not bowing to the gold image of King Nebuchadnezzar. And when the king looked in the flames, he saw four men loosed and walking around. When the three men finally came out, they were unharmed and the bounds were burned off, but not even the smell of fire was on them (Daniel 3:23-27). God used that story to explain to me that we go through the fires because He is burning off what binds us, so we can walk in freedom. However, He gives us two promises when we do experience a Job season: 1) He will be with us even in the fires (scholars believe the fourth person in the furnace symbolized the Presence of God) and 2) Not even the smell of smoke will linger, meaning God will absolutely eradicate the scent of evil we experienced, and we will be left with only His blessings and our character arc.

Discussion or Journal Question

Character arcs are important in books, movies and definitely in life. We are becoming the people we will be for eternity, and the difficulties of life transform us in the best image God has for us. We grow and mature as we face obstacles and overcome them. Can you think of a difficult obstacle you faced that forced you to overcome, allowing you to grow stronger in your faith, understanding and compassion? Write your answer below or discuss with a group.

Age of Noah

The Great Reset

God is outside of time. Like watching a parade from a high building, God sees the beginning of time to the end simultaneously. He is no longer creating in this world. He created the seeds to continue all creation during the first six days to perpetuate life through the fruition of time. Now He is watching and moving as time grows to maturity until the moment of Jesus' second return and final reign. Just like the series, *Lord of the Rings*, by J.R.R. Tolkien, has four ages, I believe the time on our earth has four ages, and we are now in the fourth age.

1. **The Age of Noah**
2. **The Age of Abraham**
3. **The Age of Moses**
4. **The Age of Paul**

The Age of Noah: The Great Reset

> *"And I will put enmity (open hostility) Between you and the woman,* ***And between your seed (offspring) and her Seed; He shall [fatally] bruise your head,*** *And you shall [only] bruise His heel"* (Genesis 3.15 AMP).

The time between Adam and Eve's exit from the Garden of Eden to the time of the Great Flood produced a plot arc filled with the stuff of legend. Needless to say, the enemy Satan was after the seed or offspring of Eve and almost succeeded in completely contaminating her bloodline with his wickedness. Satan knew that from Eve the Messiah would come, and Jesus would fatally crush him; so he and his demons did everything possible to stop God's abysmal forecast for his future from coming to pass. Between chapter 4 and chapter 7 of Genesis,

49

humankind experienced a rapid decline until God grieved and was sorry He made had them (Genesis 6.6). However, because of God's great grace (Genesis 6.8), He chose Noah, a righteous man (meaning he walked in relationship with God and had faith in His voice, like Abraham), to be a seed for a new era.

> *"This is the account of Noah and his family. Noah was a righteous man, the only blameless person living on earth at the time, and he walked in close fellowship with God"* (Genesis 6.9 NLT).

Noah built an Ark by faith, and God finally unleashed the rains. Only Noah, his family and the animals in the Ark were saved from the Great Flood. Every physical aspect of creation on land (plants, animals and humans) was destroyed—though, we know that the spiritual entities continued to exist (angels and demons) because the other three ages of time contain stories that involve both angels and demons.

The Great Flood destroyed the physical world, but notably, the dormant seeds of vegetation were saved because new growth outside the Ark occurred after the waters receded (Genesis 8.11). And assumedly, the fish of the sea survived since they were water bound, not bound to the ground of the earth.

> *"So He destroyed all living things which were on the face of the ground: both man and cattle, creeping thing and bird of the air. They were destroyed from the earth. Only Noah and those who were with him in the ark remained alive. And the waters prevailed on the earth one hundred and fifty days"* (Genesis 7.23-24 NKJV).

There are many books that delve into this first age, but the main takeaway that I want to focus on is that nothing is too lost to be saved by God. Many times, God will send great floods into our lives to wash away everything not rooted in Him. The situation, the problem or the person is never too far gone for God to rescue. The Ark can be a metaphor for Jesus. Just as Noah, his family and the animals had to go through the door of the Ark to be saved, we are saved through the Door of Christ (John 10.7 ESV). Thankfully, just like in the story of Job, God offers us a fresh start even though it may seem like all is lost. And this fresh start now occurs in time as we go into the next age. The last three ages are what I want to focus on the most regarding grace fulfilling law.

The Three Ages

Pre-Law Righteous by Faith & Relationship	Law (613) Righteous by Obedience & Sacrifices	Post-Law Righteous by Faith & Grace
Belief Based God Focused Friend of God	Performance Based Sin Focused Slave to Sin	Belief Based Jesus Focused Child of God
One Commandment ↑ Genesis 2.16-17	Many Commandments ↑ Exodus 20.1-17 *Final Sacrifice*	One Commandment ↑ Matthew 22.37-39
Age of Abraham "Baby Heir" Covenant of Faith	Age of Moses "Child Heir" Covenant of Guardianship	Age of Paul "Adult Heir" Covenant of Grace

I created the above image as a visual aid for us to understand how time is maturing until the return of Jesus at the closing of the fourth age where we will finally dwell outside of time in eternity. Although, this image is simplified (there are so many more details I can fit into each age), but this is a good starting point. I believe that as we mature, time is also maturing in a temporal womb until it is born into eternity, and we get our New Earth and New Heaven. Just like we will be given new bodies when we die (Philippians 3.21), the earth will be given a new "body" in eternity.

> *"Then I saw a new heaven and a new earth, for the old heaven and the old earth had disappeared. And the sea was also gone"* (Revelation 21.1 NLT).

We can parallel the maturing of time to our own spiritual maturing. We are made up of three parts: body, soul and spirit. Our body is our physical design by God shaped by the unfolding of our lives. Our soul— composed of our mind (thoughts and imaginings), our heart (feelings and emotions) and our will (actions and choices)—is our metaphysical design by God shaped by the unfolding of our lives. Finally, our spirit is rooted outside of time in eternity. This part of us is eternal and is either dead (separated from God) or alive (united with God). Once we accept Jesus as our Lord and Savior, the spiritual part of us comes to life because now we have righteousness through Christ (Romans 3.22), and we can be united with God. Paul's words below explain this truth well:

> *"And you were dead in the trespasses and sins in which you once walked, following the course of this world, following the prince of the power of the air, the spirit that is now at work in the sons of disobedience— among whom we all once lived in the passions of our flesh, carrying out the desires of the body and the mind, and were by nature children of wrath, like the rest of mankind. But God, being rich in mercy, because of the great love with which he loved us, even when we were dead in our trespasses, made us alive together*

with Christ—by grace you have been saved—and raised us up with him and seated us with him in the heavenly places in Christ Jesus" (Ephesians 2.1-6 ESV).

Being "born again" alludes to a birth of our spirit. Jesus explained this truth to the Pharisee Nicodemus that we must have two births: flesh and spirit.

"That which is born of the flesh is flesh, and that which is born of the Spirit is spirit. Do not marvel that I said to you, 'You must be born again.' The wind blows where it wishes, and you hear its sound, but you do not know where it comes from or where it goes. So it is with everyone who is born of the Spirit" (John 3.6-8 ESV).

Once we accept Jesus' Sacrifice on the Cross as payment for our sins, our spirit can now be seated with Christ in heaven. At any moment, when our body dies, we will be in God's Presence. However, God does not take us home right away because He wants to work that gift of perfection and righteousness of our spirit (given to us freely by grace and received freely by faith) into our body and soul, producing an overflow of good works on earth that will come with us to eternity.

That is where the maturing comes in. When we are saved through Jesus Christ, we are yet like babies who need to be nurtured. Then we become like children who need to be guided. Finally, we become like adults who can nurture and guide others (though, we will continually grow in the Lord until our death on this earth). This is true for time as well. Time has nurtured humanity through the Age of Abraham. It has guided humanity through the Age of Moses. Finally, we live in the time of Sabbath Rest because of the Cross, and now we can produce good works like Jesus during the Age of Paul (John 14.12-14).

Satan's evil schemes continued through each age, but now he knows he has lost in this final fourth age. Jesus overcame the world, taking back all authority, so Satan and his evil demons must scheme to prevent us from knowing that we too have the victory in Christ (John 16.33, Matthew 28.18 & 1 Corinthians 15.57). Satan is a sore loser, and he wants to distract us from our destiny and prevent us from producing good works with the authority given to us by Jesus. Satan couldn't stop Jesus from having the final victory (though, he desperately tried during the first three ages), but he is doing everything he can now to prevent that victory from being known in this final age. But we don't have to fret. Jesus said that we can depend on him until the end.

> *"And be sure of this: I am with you always, even to the end of the age"* (Matthew 28.20 NLT).

Let us take a brief look at each age, so we can gain a fuller understanding of how grace fulfills the laws. Then we will tie all the ages back to Job, and his need for a Mediator. Finally, we will discover that because of Jesus, all the commandments given to us by God through Moses can be boiled down to one: loving God, loving others and loving ourselves.

Discussion or Journal Question

Noah's Rainbow is symbolic of second chances (Genesis 9.8-11). Have you experienced a time in your life or in a loved one's life where God opened a door for an extra chance against all odds? Did that time include moments of miracles only God could perform? Write your answer below or discuss with a group.

Age of Abraham

Baby to Toddler

*"For what does the Scripture say? **'Abraham believed God, and it was counted to him as righteousness'"** (Romans 4.3 ESV).*

The Covenant of Faith

During the Age of Abraham, the Law of Moses had not been established. We are still left with the single command from the Garden of Eden not to eat from the Tree of Knowledge of Good and Evil (Genesis 2.16-17), which equates to our free will to obey or not to obey God according to what we know to be good and to our growing intimacy with

Him. Abraham was a friend of God, and he shared his life journey with Him.

> *"And so it happened just as the Scriptures say: 'Abraham believed God, and God counted him as righteous because of his faith.' He was even called the **friend of God**"* (James 2.23 NLT).

Abraham walked in close relationship with God. There were no other established laws to condemn him except for obeying the conscience encoded in him because he was designed in the image of God (both material and immaterial aspects of that design), and he walked with Him (Genesis 1.26-27 & Genesis 17.1). In essence, it means choosing not to eat of the Tree of Knowledge of Good and Evil (the one command given in the Garden of Eden), according to what we know to be right and wrong as we walk in relationship with God. Paul explains this inner conscience best:

> *"Even Gentiles, who do not have God's written law, **show that they***

know his law when they instinctively obey it, even without having heard it. They demonstrate that **God's law is written in their hearts**, for their own conscience and thoughts either accuse them or tell them they are doing right" (Romans 2.14-15 NLT).

I liken the Age of Abraham to the time a baby is born until the point he or she reaches the age of accountability. They don't know the rules of the home or community, but as they walk in relationship with their mothers and fathers, their worldview is being formed. If they break a rule, like touching a hot iron, they will feel the consequences; yet they are not accountable if the rule was never made known. The toddler is too young to memorize a bunch of rules, so the parents and caregivers must walk alongside the child in a close relationship to nurture intimacy and establish the difference between what is good for the child and what is not. The child knows only one rule once they grow out of infancy: to obey Mom and Dad; and when they disobey, they know they have made the wrong choice.

Abraham was considered righteous not because he followed a bunch of rules; but rather, he followed his God daily. He was righteous because he believed God and his belief created obedient steps of faith. God told him to leave his home, and he obeyed (Genesis 12.1). God told him to bring five animals for sacrifice, and he obeyed (Genesis 15.9-10). God told him to sacrifice his son, and he obeyed (though, God saved him from the ultimate execution of that step of obedience) (Genesis 22.1-19).

However, Abraham wasn't perfect. He lied about his wife being only his sister (she was his half-sister) and didn't admit that she was also his wife to King Abimelech of Gerar (Genesis 20.12). Abraham's lie risked the lives of the king and his nation. Though this king did not walk with God, even he knew what Abraham did was wrong.

> *"Then Abimelech called for Abraham. 'What have you done to us?' he demanded. "What crime have I committed that deserves treatment*

*like this, making me and my kingdom guilty of this great sin? **No one should ever do what you have done!** Whatever possessed you to do such a thing?'"* (Genesis 20.9-10 NLT).

Abraham also didn't wait on God and had a son out of wedlock and without God's permission (Genesis 16.2-4). Even though Abraham made mistakes and did things he knew were wrong, God still fulfilled His promise to Abraham for a child with Sarah who would become the seed of nations (Genesis 17.4 & Genesis 21.1-2). Abraham's righteousness was not based on his performance; it was based on his belief. The Law of Moses had not been established, so it could not condemn him, nor did God. In fact, God wanted to greatly bless Abraham (Genesis 12.2-3), despite his shortcomings, because he believed God's voice like a toddler would believe his father's voice.

*"And **he believed in the LORD**, and He accounted it to him for righteousness"* (Genesis 15.6 NKJV).

Slaying Job | Alisa Hope Wagner

Toddlers are like Abraham in that they believe everything their parents say to be true—even though they may disobey at times. Even in Abraham's old age, he believed that God would give him his promised son. That is why Jesus directed us to become like little children (Matthew 18.2-4). We must take every word and promise of God and make it truth in our hearts, despite our circumstances, feelings and the voices of others around us. Our faith in God above all else pleases Him (Hebrews 11.6). Faith is not a feeling. It is a choice.

> *"Even when there was no reason for hope, Abraham kept hoping—believing that he would become the father of many nations. For God had said to him, 'That's how many descendants you will have!' And Abraham's faith did not weaken, even though, at about 100 years of age, he figured his body was as good as dead—and so was Sarah's womb.* **Abraham never wavered in believing God's promise.** *In fact, his faith grew stronger, and in this he*

*brought glory to God. **He was fully convinced that God is able to do whatever he promises**"* (Romans 4.18-21 NLT).

The Age of Abraham occurred before the Law of Moses. Righteousness was gained by faith through an intimate life-walk with God. Belief in God directed the steps of the individual. The Mediator, Jesus, had not yet accomplished the Law of Grace because the Law of Moses had not yet been established. This age can be likened to the years of a baby to a toddler—ignorant of the commandments and complete dependency on a relationship with God. But as we will soon discover, the next age (that I liken to the ages of a child to a teenager) the commandments will be established, like street signs of dos and don'ts littering the earth. Instead of looking to our Heavenly Father for daily guidance, we will be burdened by keeping in-step with the numerous rules of the home and community. And since we now know the rules, we are held accountable to keep them.

Slaying Job | Alisa Hope Wagner

We now become aware of our sin, and that sin condemns us.

> "Now we know that whatever the law says it speaks to those who are under the law, so that every mouth may be stopped, and the **whole world may be held accountable to God**. For by works of the law no human being will be justified in his sight, since through the law comes knowledge of sin" (Romans 3.19-20 ESV).

Therefore, along with the Law of Moses, a routine of offerings (sacrifices) found in Leviticus 1-7 had to be established to atone for breaking the laws. Jesus said Himself: *"Has not Moses given you the law? Yet not one of you keeps the law"* (John 7.19a NIV). God knew we would never be able to keep the laws, but He also knew that this realization would move us away from relying on our own counterfeit righteousness and trusting in the Finished Work of Jesus on the Cross. This is the same lesson Job learned when he lost everything. Thankfully for us,

Slaying Job | Alisa Hope Wagner

we live in the final Age of Paul where Jesus gave us His righteousness freely.

Slaying Job | Alisa Hope Wagner

Discussion or Journal Question

Walking with God is a daily choice to spend time with Him and to read His Word. Intimacy takes effort, and what we prioritize we will always accomplish. How can you make small changes in your life to prioritize your relationship with God? How does spending time with Him give you rest from the daily grind of life and offer you freedom from the traps of the enemy? Write your answer below or discuss with a group.

Age of Moses

Child to Teenager

"So the **law was our guardian** until Christ came that we might be justified by faith" (Galatians 3.24 NIV).

The Covenant of Guardianship

Now time is about to mature to its childhood and teenage years during the Age of Moses. The twelve tribes of Israel are finally out of the shackles of slavery in Egypt. God prophesied to Abraham their 400-year enslavement, but He also added that they would leave that land with great wealth, which would become the seed for them to form their own nation in their own Promised Land (Genesis 15.13-14). They left slavery rich and began following God by a Pillar of Cloud by day and a Pillar of Fire by night while they wandered the wilderness (Exodus 13.21-22).

God wanted one thing from His people. He brought them to Himself because He longed for a covenant of relationship with them like He had with their forefathers: Abraham, Isaac and Jacob. He wanted them to listen to His voice and obey Him in a relational way, so He could bless them above all people.

> "And Moses went up to God, and the LORD called to him from the mountain, saying, 'Thus you shall say to the house of Jacob, and tell the children of Israel: "You have seen what I did to the Egyptians, and *how* **I bore you on eagles' wings and brought you to Myself. Now therefore, if you will indeed obey My voice and keep My covenant, then you shall be a special treasure to Me above all people; for all the**

earth *is* Mine. And you shall be to Me a kingdom of priests and a holy nation." These *are* the words which you shall speak to the children of Israel'" (Exodus 19.3-6 NKJV).

When God commanded that they listen to His voice and keep a covenant of relationship with Him, they asserted that they would obey: *"Then all the people answered together and said, 'All that the LORD has spoken we will do'"* (Exodus 19.8 NKJV). Finally, Moses tells the people to prepare to meet their God. They must have been so excited for Moses to introduce them and to have a relationship with Him like Moses did, but sadly their fear overpowered their excitement.

> *"And Moses brought the people out of the camp to meet with God, and they stood at the foot of the mountain"* (Exodus 19. 17 NKJV).

They consecrated themselves, so on the third day, the Lord could come to them

(Exodus 19.10-11). However, there was thunder, lightning, lots of smoke and loud sounds of trumpets; and the people were scared and stood at a distance (Exodus 20.18). They feared God because they have not walked in intimacy with Him. They broke their promise to obey and did not want to come to Him and listen to His voice.

A child who walks in intimacy with her mother and father will trust them even during scary circumstances. In fact, she would rather walk into the thunderstorm with her parents, hand-in-hand, than be left behind at a safe distance without them. God tested His people and they failed miserably (Exodus 20.20). They demanded to stay behind and only Moses went up. The people did not want to have a personal relationship with God. They did not want to speak with Him face to face like Moses (Exodus 33.11). Therefore, the Age of Abraham was replaced with laws during the Age of Moses.

> *"Then they said to Moses, 'You speak with us, and we will hear;* **but let not God speak with us,** *lest we die'"* (Exodus 20.19 NKJV).

Slaying Job | Alisa Hope Wagner

Instead, like older children and teenagers pulling away from parental guidance, they don't want to listen to their parents' voices. This will free the teenagers from having to constantly rely on Mom and Dad. If they simply knew the rules of the house, they would obey them, not the voices of their parents. Therefore, daily interaction would not be necessary. The only problem is that teenagers are still young and make many mistakes. Mom and Dad will have to continue a relationship with their child or teen—even if only to correct, punish and admonish.

Starting with the first Ten Commandments, Moses offers 613 laws for the home and community. Now our one commandment (to simply obey the voice of God as we walk in relationship with Him) had become many. Since the laws have been established on Earth, we are now accountable to follow them. If we break even one, we fall short of them all. Therefore, The Five Offerings of Leviticus 1-7 were established to make up for our shortcomings.

Slaying Job | Alisa Hope Wagner

1. The Burnt Offering
2. The Meal Offering
3. The Peace Offering
4. The Sin Offering
5. The Trespass Offering

Instead of looking to God and obeying His voice, we turn our focus to looking at the laws and obeying them and giving offerings when we fail. Instead of intimacy, we now have performance. The laws become like guardians or boundaries to us, directing our steps according to the dos and don'ts of the laws. And no matter how hard we try, the laws only condemn us, constantly reminding us that we will always fall short of God's perfect standard (Romans 3.23).

Paul describes this point best in Galatians 4. This segment of verses is long, but it does a great job of showing the evolution of time. When the Law of Moses was given, it was like a death of the relationship we had with our God during the Age of Abraham. The laws became our guardians until the time our inheritance (Jesus the Messiah) would come and fulfill the laws on our behalf, so we could be reconciled to our Father again and receive once more a single commandment of love.

> *"Think of it this way. **If a father dies and leaves an inheritance for his young children**, those children are not much better off than slaves until they grow up, even though they actually own everything their father had. **They have to obey their guardians until they reach whatever age their father set**. And that's the way it was with us before Christ came. We were like children; we were slaves to the basic spiritual principles of this world. But when the right time came, God sent his Son, born of a woman, subject to the law. **God sent him to buy freedom for us who were slaves to the law, so that he could adopt us as his very own children.** And because we are his children, God has sent the Spirit of his Son into our hearts, prompting us to call out, 'Abba, Father.' Now you are no longer a slave but God's own child.*

And since you are his child, God has made you his heir" (Galatians 4.1-7 NLT).

It is interesting to note that the Law of Moses was given fifty days after the first Passover in Egypt when the Angel of Death passed over every house with the lamb's blood painted on the doorpost (Exodus 12.23-36). Once the Law of Moses was given, Moses found that the people of God had created a golden calf and called it their god and built an alter to it and gave it offerings (Exodus 32.4-6). Moses broke the tablets that had the laws written on them, and three thousand people died that day.

On the contrary, we will find that in the Age of Paul that fifty days after Jesus' Sacrifice on the Cross (which occurred on Passover because He is our final Passover Lamb, and His blood allows the Angel of Death to pass over us), the Holy Spirit was unleashed onto the Earth on Pentecost, and three thousand people were saved by the power of the Holy Spirit speaking through Peter (Acts 2.38-41). The laws enslave and condemn. However, grace frees and forgives.

Moses had it right when he talked to God face-to-face. He expressed that he wouldn't go anywhere without God's Presence going with him. Moses wanted God to "show" him His ways, not simply set a bunch of stringent rules to follow. Like Abraham, Moses found grace in God's eyes because he longed to be in a covenant relationship with Him (Exodus 33.17). And that is what God wants from all of us. He longs for an intimate relationship, and He allowed the laws for a time to show us how much we need Him daily. The laws also became the segue for Jesus to enter Earth when people so desperately saw their need for the Messiah because they were so aware of their sins.

> "Now therefore, I pray, if I have found grace in Your sight, **show me now Your way, that I may know You and that I may find grace in Your sight**. And consider that this nation is Your people.' And He said, 'My Presence will go with you, and I will give you

rest.' Then he said to Him, *'If Your Presence does not go with us, do not bring us up from here. For how then will it be known that Your people and I have found grace in Your sight, except You go with us?* So we shall be separate, Your people and I, from all the people who are upon the face of the earth"* (Exodus 33.13-16 NKJV).

Discussion or Journal Question

It is easy to get caught up in trying to prove our righteousness to others and ourselves. In fact, we can become so sin-focused by the laws that we back ourselves into a corner of fear to the point that we cannot be used by God to reach others with the love of Christ. Can you think of a time when you missed an opportunity to touch someone's life with God's love because of fear of being judged? Or is there a time where you showed love despite the judgments of others? Write your answer below or discuss with a group.

Age of Paul

Young Adult to Adult

> *"Sin is no longer your master, for you no longer live under the requirements of the law. Instead, **you live under the freedom of God's grace**"* (Romans 6.14 NLT).

The Covenant of Grace

Now we are in the Age of Paul because of what the Lamb of God has accomplished on our behalf. The prophets of the Old Testament prophesied about the coming of the Messiah and His ultimate victory. One of the most notable prophecies of Jesus was beautifully penned by the poet and prophet, Isaiah.

> *"But he was pierced for our rebellion, crushed for our sins. He was beaten so we could be whole. He was whipped so we could be healed. All of us, like sheep, have strayed away. We have left God's paths to follow our own.* **Yet the LORD laid on him the sins of us all**" (Isaiah 53.5-6 NLT).

Satan has lost. Sin has been atoned for. The Devil could not destroy the offspring of Eve, Jesus, Who would eventually crush him. Satan's time is limited, so his main focus now is to prevent people from knowing the truth about Jesus our Messiah, Who took the sins of the world on His shoulders and gave us His righteousness. At this very moment, if we have accepted the final Passover Lamb as our Lord and Savior, we stand holy and blameless before all heaven and earth, and the devil has absolutely no right to condemn, accuse and shame us.

What is even more awesome is that Jesus fulfilled the rigorous requirements of the laws according to God's holy standard, not simply the human standards given through the Law of Moses. Jesus accomplished the laws beyond physical performance. He accomplished it in His will (actions and choices), mind (thoughts and imaginings) and heart (feelings and emotions). Jesus talked to His disciples about the Law of Moses, and He gave them a holier level of God's righteous standard that would be impossible for any of us to keep.

In the Book of Matthew chapter 5 verses 17-43, Jesus laid down the holiest expectation of a perfect God. This was the standard we must keep to be in God's Presence. Jesus did not come to erase this standard; He came to accomplish it for us, so we could live under a single law once more.

> *"Don't misunderstand why I have come. I did not come to abolish the law of Moses or the writings of the prophets. **No, I came to accomplish their purpose**"* (Matthew 5.17 NLT).

Jesus explained it this way. One of the laws given by Moses was do not murder

(Exodus 20.13). Yet, Jesus brought this command to the highest level. He said if we are merely angry with someone, we stand condemned by God's holy standard (Matthew 5.22). Another law of Moses was do not commit adultery (Exodus 20.14). However, Jesus brought this command to the highest level. He said if we lust after another person other than our spouse, we stand condemned (Matthew 5.28). Yet another law of Moses was that a man can simply give his wife a certificate of divorce if she displeases him (Deuteronomy 24.1). On the contrary, Jesus said this law was only given as a concession to men because of their "hard hearts." The highest level of marriage would be to stay united as one as it was intended in the Garden of Eden (Genesis 2.24).

> *"Jesus replied, 'Moses permitted divorce only as a concession to your hard hearts, but it was not what God had originally intended'"* (Matthew 19.8 NLT).

Slaying Job | Alisa Hope Wagner

Jesus fulfilled the highest standard of the laws on our behalf, becoming our inheritance and moving us into the final Age of Paul which allows us to be righteous by faith once more because His grace accomplished the laws. Abraham was righteous because he walked by faith before the Law of Moses was established. Now we are righteous because we walk by faith, and since the laws were established, grace has to flow from the Lamb of God, achieving the holy standard on our behalf.

> "For **Christ has already accomplished the purpose for which the law was given**. *As a result, all who believe in him are made right with God*" (Romans 10.4 NLT).

Therefore, the Age of Paul is of both faith and grace. Now, like in the Age of Abraham, we are back to a single commandment that encompasses all the laws in one: to love God, others and ourselves.

"Jesus replied, 'You must love the **LORD your <u>God</u>** *with all your heart, all your soul, and all your mind.' This is the first and greatest commandment. A second is equally important:* **'Love your <u>neighbor</u> as <u>yourself</u>.' The entire law and all the demands of the prophets are based on these two commandments"** (Matthew 22.37-40 NLT).

Time has moved from adolescence to adulthood in the Age of Paul. We no longer need the Covenant of Guardianship with the Law of Moses because we have the Covenant of Grace with Jesus by faith. We finally have our inheritance, the Messiah. Like a good Father, God is telling us that He trusts us as adults. A parent wants to lift the rules of the home, establishing an atmosphere of love and trust when a child has grown into adulthood. Once a young adult reaches a certain age, the love, truth and intimacy we nurtured that child in will help him make the right choices. Yes, he will definitely make mistakes (with freedom comes slips), but he will never fully mature if we oppress him with rules that stifle his ability to discern and learn for himself. And if he loves and respects us as a loving parent, he will want to choose wisely, not because he has to but because he wants to.

Spouse of Grace

> *"So, my brothers and sisters, **you also died to the law through the body of Christ**, that you might belong to another, to him who was raised from the dead, in order that we might bear fruit for God. For when we were in the realm of the flesh, the sinful passions aroused by the law were at work in us, so that we bore fruit for death. **But now, by dying to what once bound us, we have been released from the law so that we serve in the new way of the Spirit**, and not in the old way of the written code"* (Romans 7.4-6 NIV).

During the Age of Moses, we were married to Mr. Law. He guarded us, condemned us and illuminated all our imperfections, so we would constantly have to give offerings and sacrifices to make up for our shortcomings. But now because of Jesus' Finished Work on the Cross, we have died in Christ, which releases us from our marriage to Mr. Law. Now we get to marry Mr. Grace. The laws have been fulfilled by Jesus via grace, and we are perfected and holy by faith. We can have God's Spirit, the Holy Spirit, guiding us each day, not rigorous rules condemning us (Galatians 5.18). Hurray! We have a new Bridegroom Who is Jesus Christ, the Messiah, and now that we are married to Mr. Grace, sin can no longer push us around and condemn us because we are bound to a Holy God in the new Covenant of Grace.

> *"For sin shall no longer be your master, because you are not under the law, but under grace"* (Romans 6.14 NIV).

This grace doesn't give us license to sin and get away with it. Would a devoted wife sin against her husband just because she knew he would always forgive her? No! This grace allows us to truly know we have been made righteous in God's eyes, and we can walk boldly to the throne of grace because Jesus makes up for our flaws and weaknesses (Hebrews 4.16). In fact, God's power is made complete in our limitations. We have hit the jackpot of all marriages! Our righteousness is not based on our own striving or merit or works. We can rest in the righteousness of Christ, and from an overflow of thankfulness and joy, we live a life in step with the Spirit, creating good works by faith, not to earn God's pleasure but to rejoice in it.

> *"But he said to me, 'My grace is sufficient for you, for my power is made perfect in weakness.' Therefore I will boast all the more gladly about my weaknesses, so that Christ's power may rest on me"* (2 Corinthians 12.9 NIV).

Discussion or Journal Question

It is easy to focus on our sins rather than the amazing grace of God through Jesus Christ. However, we must ask ourselves which is more powerful: the laws that condemn us or Jesus' love that forgives us? Are you carrying around regret, shame and guilt from past mistakes or hurts? How can knowing that you are righteous in God's eyes through Jesus free you from condemnation? Write your answer below or discuss with a group.

The Final Sacrifice

Jesus Fulfills the Laws

"For the Law was given through
Moses, but grace [the unearned,
undeserved favor of God] and truth
came through Jesus Christ" (John
1.17 AMP).

God gave us free will in the Garden of
Eden, which is why He created an extra tree
(Jesus, the Tree of Life) and an extra day (the
Seventh Day of Sabbath). God, our Creator,
rested, knowing that Jesus would
accomplish the work of reconciling the world
back to Himself by becoming the Final
Sacrifice, the Lamb of God, offered to atone
for the sins of the world (Hebrews 10.12-14).

Slaying Job | Alisa Hope Wagner

After so many years of living with Mr. Law and focusing on all 613 laws plus the hundreds of human-made rules that came out of those laws, time was ready to introduce us to Jesus via His birth into this world. We were ready because we realized how utterly helpless we were to save ourselves. Now instead of being scared to enter into a relationship with God like in the Age of Moses, we cry out for a Messiah to bring us back to God in the Age of Paul, a time of Sabbath Rest.

> *"When we were utterly helpless, Christ came at just the right time and died for us sinners"* (Romans 5.6 NLT).

This truth was difficult for religious leaders of Jesus' time to accept. They liked being married to Mr. Law because they could be righteous in their own eyes. They didn't have to rely on an intimate, daily relationship with God. They didn't have to show mercy and love to others and get their feet dirty serving them. They simply obeyed the house rules and gave their offerings, but their hearts were far from God. Jesus did not have kind words to say to the people who were wise in their own eyes—a problem Job had before He went through the fires of his struggle to truly "see" God. Jesus said the following to the religious leaders:

> "You hypocrites! Isaiah was right when he prophesied about you: **'These people honor me with their lips, but their hearts are far from me. They worship me in vain; their teachings are merely human rules'"** (Matthew 15.7-9 NIV).

Their teachings were rules created by humans based on the Law of Moses, but all God truly wanted was a Covenant of relationship with His beloved people, so we may hear His voice and obey Him, like Abraham did. And God accomplished this on the Seventh Day of Sabbath Rest through the Final Sacrifice of the Lamb of God, His Son, Jesus the Messiah. We don't have to be like pre-struggle Job, constantly sin-focused and striving to give sacrifices for the what-ifs of sin. We can be like post-struggle Job, resting in grace and loving others and God in intimate, daily relationships.

Sabbath Rest

> "Then he said to them, 'The Sabbath was made for man, not man for the Sabbath. So the Son of Man is Lord even of the Sabbath'" (Mark 2.27 NIV).

Sabbath Rest is not simply a day. It is a state of mind. It is the era in which we live. And it is a choice we can make daily. God created it for us as a gift, so we could be reconciled back to Him through Jesus where rest, peace and joy dwell continuously. He did not create the Sabbath to be overflowing with a bunch of rules. Just one: Love God, others and ourselves (Mark 12.30-31). Just like Job had to struggle to get into his rest, we must struggle to get into the Sabbath Rest of Jesus. It's freely available because we live in the Age of Paul after the Final Sacrifice, but it takes dying to self – our frustrations, our desires, our goals, our efforts, our agendas, our heartaches, and, yes, even our traumas – and living in Christ, trusting He will provide everything we need as we seek Him (Luke 9.23, 1 John 5.20 & Matthew 6.33).

This trust will not always be a feeling. In fact, as we mature in Christ, we many times must walk by what we know to be true—that God is with us always—even when we don't feel like He is there (Joshua 1.9). This is what it means to walk by faith and not sight, which is why reading our Bibles and praying daily is so imperative (2 Corinthians 5.7). All God's promises are potentially ours—meaning we can't claim what we don't know.

You can't claim God's promise of peace through Jesus unless you know that it is available to you (John 14.27). You can't claim God's promise of healing through Jesus unless you know it is available to you (1 Peter 2.24). You can't claim God's promise of victory through Jesus unless you know it is available to you (1 Corinthians 15.57). There are so many promises we have through Jesus, but we must know them to claim them. And Sabbath Rest is one of the biggest promises to us through Jesus, but we must wrestle to get there as Paul explains.

> *"Therefore, since the **promise of entering his rest still stands**, let us be careful that none of you be found to have fallen short of it...There remains, then, **a Sabbath-rest for the people of God; for anyone who enters God's rest also rests from their works, just as God did from his**. Let us, therefore, make every **effort to enter that rest**..."* Hebrews 4.1 & Hebrews 4.9-11 NIV).

God's rest is a promise to us. It is potentially ours if we claim it. Isn't it strange that we must make an effort to enter into God's Sabbath Rest? And what will that effort entail? I believe the number one thing that keeps us from entering God's rest is striving to be righteous in our own eyes and in the eyes of others. That is what it means to daily die to self and take up our cross.

> *"Then Jesus told his disciples, 'If anyone would come after me, **let him***

deny himself and take up his cross
and follow me" (Matthew 16.24 ESV).

I have personally struggled with trying to be righteous in my own eyes and in the eyes of others, and that striving almost drove me mad. But if you look at the life of Jesus, He was constantly offending the "righteous" leaders of His time. He ate with sinners (Luke 15.1-2). He went to Zacchaeus's house, a tax collector who was despised because he was considered a traitor (Luke 19.5). He talked to a Samaritan woman (also despised because of her race), and Jesus and she were alone together, and she had multiple husbands, which would be seen as an extremely inappropriate meeting (John 4.7-30). And He let a woman notorious for sinning touch Him and pour expensive perfume on His feet (Luke 7.36-50). He didn't have to prove His righteousness to the people because He was God in the flesh, walking among us.

"Look! The virgin will conceive a
child! She will give birth to a son, and

they will call him Immanuel, which means 'God is with us'" (Matthew 1.23 NLT).

We don't have to prove our righteousness either because we are the righteousness of God through Jesus Christ (Romans 3.22). Once we quit trying to prove we are righteous to ourselves and others and finally realize we ARE righteous through Jesus, we will finally find our rest in God. We will hear His voice daily and follow Him. And when we make mistakes, which of course we will, we can repent and rebuke any condemnation that the enemy, others and even ourselves try to shame us with (Romans 8.1-3).

In fact, the enemy has already lost. He has nothing for which to condemn us because our sins have been forgiven. We stand righteous and holy before all of Heaven and Earth, and literally *we are rubber, and he is glue;* anything the enemy speaks against us (lies, accusations, condemnation, sickness, lack, depression, anxiety, etc.) bounces off us and sticks to him! We live in the Age of Paul and of

Slaying Job | Alisa Hope Wagner

Sabbath Rest. The Final Sacrifice of the Lamb of God has been made, and we have the victory. Jesus is our everything because He gave us Himself.

"Thank You, Jesus, for allowing Yourself to be forsaken by God, so we could be reconciled back to Him (Matthew 27.46). You may have given up Your life for us, but You had the power to take it back up again. You took our sins into the grave and left them there. We have died in You, and now Mr. Law can no longer condemn us. At this very moment, our spirit is alive and dwells in You at the right-hand side of God (John 10.18 & Colossians 3.1). I dedicate the following poem to You, my Lord and Savior, Jesus the Messiah."

The Alphabet of Jesus
Alisa Hope Wagner

My Award.
My Best.
My Clarity.
My Divinity.
My Energy.
My Freedom.
My God.
My Healing.
My Integrity.
My Joy.
My Kindness.
My Love.
My Miracle.
My Nobility.
My Obedience.
My Perfection.
My Quiet.
My Redemption.
My Strength.
My Truth.

Slaying Job | Alisa Hope Wagner

My Understanding.
My Victory.
My Way.
My Xerox.
My Youth.
My Zeal.

Discussion or Journal Question

We live in the Age of Paul when we have the victory over the devil because Jesus crushed his head through His Finished Work on the Cross. How does knowing that we are on the winning side give you courage to resist the devil and walk in boldness? What areas in your life have you been avoiding that you can now face with God's winning strength and authority on your side? Write your answer below or discuss with a group.

The Fourth Friend

Expectancy and Experience

A fourth speaker in the *Book of Job* finally made his entrance once the dialogue between Job and his other three friends ended. This young man's name was Elihu, and he had been silent for thirty-one chapters while Job defended his innocence. Then for five chapters, Elihu justified God's actions because Job had only been trying to justify his own (Job 32.2). Once Elihu finished speaking, God finally intervened, and Job repented of being wise in his own eyes. The Bible says that God's anger burned against Job's first three friends for not speaking the truth about Him (Job 42.7), so what made Elihu so different? Why were his words the entrance point for God's speech to Job and Job's ultimate repentance?

Elihu admits that he was a young man, which was why he waited for the older men to speak (Job 32.4). His father was Barachel the Buzite who may have been a descendant of Abraham's family line. Abraham had two brothers: Nahor and Haran. Haran was the father of Lot. Haran died, so Lot went to live with his uncle, Abraham (Genesis 11.27-28 & Genesis 12.4). Abraham's other brother, Nahor, was the father of eight sons—the second born was named Buz and the baby of the family was Betheul who happened to be the father of Rebekah who married Isaac, Abraham's promised son (Genesis 20.21-23 & Genesis 24.67). Elihu may have been a descendent of Abraham's family line because his father, Barachel, was a Buzite of the lineage of Buz, Abraham's nephew.

More was known about Elihu than about Job himself, which makes me wonder if the story of Job was passed down by Elihu until finally written down by Moses or another descendent. And if the story of Job was so famous to be included in the Bible, why was there not much written about Job's ancestry? Here is where I'm going with this line of questioning. I believe Job and Elihu are one and the same—if not physically, at least symbolically. Just as Naomi, which means "my delight," changed her name to Mara, which means "bitterness," when she lost everything (Ruth 1.20); I believe Elihu, which means "He is my God," changed his name to Job, which means "hated," when he lost everything. Name changing was very common in the Bible to describe a person's current or potential position. And since the story focused more on Job's current position of wrestling with God, the title of the book aptly reflects that truth.

Job's friends could not help Job because their minds were also closed off to a true relational love of God. Job could not help himself because he may have *"forsaken the love [he] had at first"* (Revelation 2.4 NIV). Finally, Elihu's youthful and vibrant words became the ultimate pressure point to break through the darkness of Job's thinking and bring light to his understanding. Maybe Job was remembering his younger years when he walked in intimacy with the

Lord. Elihu claimed to be just like Job, being taken from the same piece of clay. Over the years, however, Job's focus turned away from relationship to striving.

> *"I am just like you before God; I was also pinched off from a piece of clay. Fear of me should not terrify you; the **pressure I exert against you will be light"** (Job 33.6-7 HCSB).

Elihu's monologue filled chapters 32 to 37 of the *Book of Job* and was awe-inspiring. I wish I could quote each word, but I at least want to highlight a few gems from the HCSB translation of the Bible.

1. *"My heart is like unvented wine; it is about to burst like new wineskins"* (Job 32.19).

Could this be a foreshadowing of Jesus' words about His Finished Work on the Cross being the New Wine of Grace? It reminds us to stop striving and to embrace God's gift of righteousness through Jesus (Matthew 9.17).

2. *"Why do you take Him to court for not answering anything a person asks? For God speaks time and again, but a person may not notice"* (Job 33.13-14).

A relationship with God is about us daily seeking Him. He is always speaking to us through His Word and World. Many times, we feel like God has abandoned us, but it is we who have not been listening.

3. *"If there is an angel on his side, one mediator out of a thousand, to tell a person what is right for him and say, 'Spare Him from going down to the Pit; I have found a ransom,' then his flesh will be healthier than in his youth, and he will return to the days of his youthful vigor"* (Job 33.23-25).

Again, we have another allusion to our Mediator, Jesus the Messiah, and it is only through Him and His righteousness that we are spared from going to the Pit.

4. *"God certainly does all these things two or three times to a man in order to turn him back from the Pit, so he may shine with light of life"* (Job 33.29-30).

God knows that it is our pride that keeps us from our loving relationship with Him, so, though He does not cause tragedy, He will use it to turn us back to Him, allowing us to experience the same test over and over again until we claim our victory.

5. *"If only Job were tested to the limit, because his answers are like those of wicked men"* (Job 34.36).

Job truly believed he was righteous and didn't deserve the difficulties of life, but his beliefs were just like people who don't have a relationship with God. Therefore, Job was "tested to the limit" to expose and transform his incorrect thinking.

6. *"If you are righteous, what do you give Him, or what does He receive from your hand"* (Job 34. 7).

God gains nothing from our efforts of perfect behavior. He wants our love. Once we give Him our love, our behavior will walk according to that love. Righteousness must be birthed out of love, not fear (1 John 4.18).

7. *"Be careful that you do not turn to iniquity, for that is why you have been tested by affliction"* (Job 36.21).

The greatest iniquity that we can commit is turning away from God and going our own way. Becoming righteous in our eyes based on our own merits causes us to think we don't need God, and we can walk away from Him—maybe not in our actions but in our hearts. Jesus died for that very sin: *"We all went astray like sheep; we all have turned to our own way; and the LORD has punished Him [Jesus] for the iniquity of us all"* (Isaiah

53.6 NIV). We must always see our need for Him.

8. *"Therefore, men fear Him. He does not look favorably on any who are wise in heart"* (Job 37.24).

God cannot use men and women who think they have nothing left to learn and who believe they are always right. God chooses the foolish, the humble and the weak to do His will (1 Corinthians 1.27). He chooses those who are last and the servants to all to be first in His kingdom (Mark 9.35).

Many years ago, as I was reading the *Book of Job*, I was confused by why Elihu, the young man with little experience in life, would be the one who would school Job on his incorrect thinking. His words sounded similar to Job's other three friends, but then the realization hit me. While Job's friends condemned Job for sinning, Elihu condemned Job for being wise in his own eyes.

Slaying Job | Alisa Hope Wagner

*"Men therefore fear Him; He does not regard nor respect any who are **wise in heart** [in their own understanding and conceit]"* (Job 37.24 AMP).

Suddenly, I had an image of Job and Elihu colliding – the expectancy of youth and the experience of age uniting as one. It was at this time that I had many disappointments in my call to write. My expectations of what I thought God was going to do through my efforts weren't coming to pass, and I was extremely discouraged. But when I saw that image of Job and Elihu colliding, I felt God ask me: *"Will you still have an expectant heart even with the experience of years of disappointments?"*

Could I continue to have the hope and excitement I had when I first began writing years later when I knew first-hand how difficult, painful and, many times, unrewarding writing was? Can my years of waiting and heartache collide with my younger self who had so much hope and belief? Would I choose to believe God's promises despite my seemingly hopeless circumstances?

And that is a question for all of us—in our calling, our marriage, our family, our finances and our health—can we still have hope in an Almighty God and His promises while we sit in a pit of darkness and despair? The single most difficult declaration we can make is to claim God's love and goodness when we don't feel or see it. However, we must be like Job who even after he lost everything and sat in the ashes, scraping at boils all over his body, was able to remember his youth (Elihu) and go back to his first love. Despite Job's hopeless circumstances, he declared His belief in God: *"I know that You can do anything and no plan of Yours can be thwarted"* (Job 42.2 HCSB). And God did it. He blessed Job's latter half of his life more than the former (Job 42.12).

Discussion or Journal Question

Have you encountered people who were so optimistic in God's love and power that they caught your notice? How did their expectant enthusiasm affect you? Or does your enthusiasm in God's unfolding glory on Earth overflow from your life onto the lives of others? Can you think of a moment when one positive word, action or choice changed the trajectory of your life or the life of someone else? Write your answer below or discuss with a group.

A Call to Love

Loving Freely in Grace

> *"But the Holy Spirit produces this kind of fruit in our lives: love, joy, peace, patience, kindness, goodness, faithfulness, gentleness, and self-control. **There is no law against these things!**"* (Galatians 5.22-23 NLT).

Love fulfills the Laws.

There is no law that can usurp the fruits of the Holy Spirit: Love, Joy, Peace, Patience, Kindness, Goodness, Faithfulness, Gentleness and Self-Control. If we have a choice between feeling self-righteous according to the laws or choosing to love, we must choose love. When we choose love, there is no law that can shame us. Jesus chose love many times, breaking several Laws of Moses. The following are only three examples, but there are many more.

Jesus touched the dead body of the girl who was not a family member; this broke the Levitical Law for Priests because He is our High Priest (Leviticus 21.1-5 & Hebrews 4:14-15). Instead, Jesus chose love and touched the girl's hand bringing her back to life (Mark 5.41-42). Moreover, when a woman was menstruating, she and everything she touched was unclean according to Levitical Law (Leviticus 15.19-20). However, Jesus allowed the woman with the twelve-year problem of bleeding to touch Him and be healed (Luke 8.43-48). Furthermore, Sabbath Rest according to Levitical Law was a day of absolutely no work (Leviticus 23.3). Yet, Jesus healed a man's crippled hand on Sabbath, creating a ruckus with the religious leaders (Mark 3.1-6). Jesus chose love above all else, and He expressed this choice in the *Parable of the Good Samaritan.*

Slaying Job | Alisa Hope Wagner

"Parable of the Good Samaritan" – Luke 10.25-37 (NIV)

> *"On one occasion an expert in the law stood up to test Jesus. 'Teacher,' he asked, 'what must I do to inherit eternal life?'*
>
> *'What is written in the Law?' he replied. 'How do you read it?'*
>
> *He answered, **'Love the Lord your <u>God</u> with all your heart and with all your soul and with all your strength and with all your mind'; and, 'Love your <u>neighbor</u> as <u>yourself</u>.'***
>
> *'You have answered correctly,' Jesus replied. 'Do this and you will live.'*
>
> *But he wanted to justify himself, so he asked Jesus, **'And who is my neighbor?'***
>
> *In reply Jesus said: 'A man was going down from Jerusalem to Jericho, when he was attacked by robbers.*

Slaying Job | Alisa Hope Wagner

*They stripped him of his clothes, beat him and went away, leaving **him half dead. A priest happened to be going down the same road, and when he saw the man, he passed by on the other side. So too, a Levite, when he came to the place and saw him, passed by on the other side. But a Samaritan, as he traveled, came where the man was; and when he saw him, he took pity on him.** He went to him and bandaged his wounds, pouring on oil and wine. Then he put the man on his own donkey, brought him to an inn and took care of him. The next day he took out two denarii and gave them to the innkeeper. "Look after him," he said, "and when I return, I will reimburse you for any extra expense you may have."'*

'Which of these three do you think was a neighbor to the man who fell into the hands of robbers?'

The expert in the law replied, 'The one who had mercy on him.'

Jesus told him, 'Go and do likewise.'"

The Levite and the Priest did not want to touch the man in case he may be dead. They didn't want to break the Levitical Law of touching a dead person who was not family because they didn't want to become unclean. But the Samaritan man (a race despised by the Jewish people because they were foreigners who intermarried with Jewish people in Samaria), took pity on the dying man and cared for him. Jesus was making a bold declaration by saying that we should act like the Samaritan who showed mercy and not like the religious leaders of the time who worried too much about appearing righteous to the point that they could not show mercy and love.

Love is a Choice

If love was merely a feeling, Jesus could not command us to love because many times we don't feel the emotion of love

(John 13.34). Love is a choice we have to make that is laid out for us in 1 Corinthians 13.4-7 (NLT), so the actions of love can be applied in practical ways.

> "**Love** *is* **patient** *and* **kind**. *Love* **is not jealous or boastful** *or* **proud** *or* **rude**. **It does not demand its own way**. *It is* **not irritable**, *and it* **keeps no record of being wronged**. *It* **does not rejoice about injustice** *but* **rejoices whenever the truth wins out**. *Love* **never gives up, never loses faith**, *is* **always hopeful**, *and* **endures through every circumstance**.

We show love by choosing to do the following with God, people and ourselves even if we don't feel like it:

1. Be Patient
2. Be Kind
3. Do Not be Jealous
4. Do Not be Boastful
5. Do Not be Proud
6. Do Not be Rude
7. Do Not Demand Your Own Way

8. Do Not be Irritable
9. Do Not Keep a Record of Wrongs
10. Do Not Rejoice in Injustice
11. Do Rejoice When Truth Wins
12. Never Give Up
13. Never Lose Faith
14. Always be Hopeful
15. Endure Every Circumstance

Every thought, choice and action we make must be filtered through the 1 Corinthians 13.4-8 verse until it becomes our nature to act according to love. Therefore, if we have a choice of looking wise in our own eyes and the eyes of others or showing love, we must always choose love. When we choose to love, we will make choices based on grace, according to the one commandment in the Age of Paul: To love God, others and ourselves. And we must make sure to extend this love to ourselves. Sometimes the most loving thing we can do is stay hopeful in our situation, yet set boundaries; be kind to ourselves, and walk away from toxic relationships; shed light to injustice, yet not rejoice in the punishment of others; not give up on a relationship yet require fair treatment; and definitely stop keeping record of all our wrongs once we have repented. Every circumstance is unique, so we must listen to the voice of God daily and read His Word for guidance.

A Choice of Faith

*"Accept the one whose faith is weak, without quarreling over disputable matters. **One person's faith allows them to eat anything, but another, whose faith is weak, eats only vegetables**. The one who eats everything must not treat with contempt the one who does not, and the one who does not eat everything must not judge the one who does, for God has accepted them…So whatever you believe about these things keep between yourself and God. **Blessed is the one who does not condemn himself by what he approves. But whoever has doubts is condemned if they eat,** because their eating is not from faith; and everything that does not come from*

faith is sin" (Romans 14.1-3 & Romans 14.22-23 NIV).

Another loving act is to not judge and condemn others or ourselves. We are all in different places in our walks of faith. Like Paul says above, *"One person's faith allows them to eat anything, but another, whose faith is weak, eats only vegetables."* We are each uniquely created by God, and He will tailor-make a walk of faith specifically for us. In essence, we must run our own race without looking to the left or right (Hebrews 12.1 & Proverbs 4.25-27). We can't compare the freedoms of others that we don't have because they also have restrictions we don't have. Plus, as we grow in our faith, our freedoms and restrictions will change according to where God is moving in our lives currently. In addition, when we judge ourselves, we give authority for the enemy to judge us. And when we judge others, we also give the enemy the right to judge us because we are standing in a counterfeit place of authority.

Slaying Job | Alisa Hope Wagner

*"Do not judge others, and you will not be judged. For you will be treated as you treat others. **The standard you use in judging is the standard by which you will be judged"** (Matthew 7.1-2 NLT).*

I had to learn to distinguish when God was convicting me of something He knew wasn't good for me or when my own heart was falsely judging me for walking in the freedom of grace. Finally, I began to build my faith over the process of years, repeating that my righteousness is in Jesus alone, so I would stop condemning myself for every little thing I did that did not appear spiritual enough to me or others. I was tired of waking up every morning with feelings of doubt and condemnation for things I knew didn't affect my faith and love of Jesus. I allowed fear of not being good enough to usurp my faith in Jesus' gift of grace. This is a terrible way to live, robbing me of my Sabbath Rest that is rightfully mine in Jesus.

Before we make any choices and actions, and as long as our choices and actions don't contradict the Bible and the

122

Holy Spirit's leading in our life, we must declare to Heaven and Earth:

> *"This choice does not affect my faith and I approve of it. I shall eat this brownie. I shall watch this movie. I shall take a tropical vacation. I shall drink a glass of wine. I shall listen to jazz music. I shall attend a cosplay party. I shall take a photo with Santa Claus. I shall buy this designer purse. This does not hurt my faith or make me less righteous. I will not judge people who do not make these choices, and they shouldn't judge me for making them. I stand righteous and holy before God, and I do not give the enemy the right to judge me. What I have chosen is between me and God, and I do not condemn myself."*

Letting Go of Perfection

Like Job, I had become a mother who was sin-focused, fearing my kids would fall into mistakes or listen, read and watch things that weren't deemed spiritual enough. And at one point, as my beautiful daughter entered adolescence, I could feel her pulling away from me. I loved her so much that I feared anything bad happening to her. What if a book she read had immoral things in it? What if a song she listened to wasn't uplifting? What if a friend she knew was a bad influence? And this list goes on and on. She couldn't be herself around me because she couldn't be perfect. I finally realized that I was losing an intimate relationship with her because of my fear. I had to choose to trust God. Life is not fair. There is pain. Kids make mistakes, but they grow from them. I would rather walk in a messy, grace-filled relationship with my daughter than a rigid, fear-filled one. Following this final chapter is a poem I wrote about how I finally learned to trust God and embrace the unknowns of life, so I could finally focus on loving my daughter in truth, not fear.

> *"**Such love has no fear, because perfect love expels all fear.** If we are afraid, it is for fear of punishment,*

and this shows that we have not fully experienced his perfect love" (1 John 4.18 NLT).

Slaying Job | Alisa Hope Wagner

Killing Perfection
Alisa Hope Wagner

I'm losing her

Childhood moments mourn
While secrets shade the soul
Can't confess to perfection
Striving steals a mother's role

Listen to what she wants
Switch to a secular station
Young hearts yearn to cry
To songs without redemption

Love can't conceal the world
And perfection fails at saving
Produces patterns of shame
With safe towers suffocating

Mistakes move adolescence
Life's troubles slide into view
Trade fear for freedom of failing

126

Slaying Job | Alisa Hope Wagner

Sheltered safeguards devastate too

Canceling my own condemnation
Insecure faults no longer hide
Grace unites my daughter to me
As perfection commits suicide

I'm finding her

Discussion or Journal Question

Loving others, especially the ones you know intimately, can be difficult and painful. Can you look back at your life and pick out a time when someone you loved didn't give up on you? Did their choice to love you despite the mess you may have created cause you to rethink your perceptions and actions? Or are there people you love who make life difficult, but you choose to love them regardless? How does choosing to love them make you more like Christ? Write your answer below or discuss with a group.

If you enjoyed this booklet, I would love for you to leave a review on Amazon. Please check out my other award-winning fiction and non-fiction books on Amazon or my blog, www.alisahopewagner.com.

www.ingramcontent.com/pod-product-compliance
Lightning Source LLC
LaVergne TN
LVHW021351080426
835508LV00020B/2224